CW01651568

The Oswestry Round

Dave Andrews and Jane Trudgill

Published by: David Andrews (Offa Books)
ISBN 978-0-9932975-0-2

Text: Dave Andrews
Photographs and map: Jane Trudgill
Email: dand103750@aol.com
Website: www.oswestryround.co.uk
Typesetting and layout design: PSCD Paul Seager Creative Design
Printed by: WPG Ltd, Welshpool

Many people have helped in the production of this book and we wish to thank all of them warmly. Firstly, we would like to thank the various friends who walked sections of the Oswestry Round, checked the route description and made valuable suggestions.

We also wish to thank Oswestry Borderland Rotary Club for their financial support and for the enthusiasm with which they have given impetus to the project. In particular we want to thank Neil Ruby for all his work on our behalf. We're very grateful to Paul Seager of PSCD for giving his time and expertise free of charge.

Thanks are due also to WPG Ltd, Welshpool. Lastly, we wish to thank our sponsors, including the Ramblers Holidays Charitable Trust, for their support. Because of the generosity shown by so many, we have been able to ensure that all royalties from the sale of this book will go to Cancer Research UK and the Lingen Davies Cancer Fund.

Contents

Introduction

The Oswestry Round is a 33-mile walking route which forms a complete circuit around the town of Oswestry. The town is in an almost unique position. To the west, the hills of the Wales-England borderland offer a rugged challenge in a beautiful setting. To the east the lower, flatter land of Shropshire is much less demanding but no less attractive.

The two major components of the route are obvious on any good map of the area. Offa's Dyke Path provides a ready-made route through the hills to the west of the town and the canal system offers an ideal route through the lower ground to the east. We have used lanes and paths that we know well as a means of connecting these two elements and completing the circle.

Because we see the Oswestry Round primarily as a 1-day walk (or run) for the very fit, it seems natural to tackle the tough, hilly sections to the west of the town first while the legs are fresh and the spirit willing. Hence the route is described anti-clockwise from its starting point at the Lion Quays complex just off the A5 to the north of Oswestry.

The route also lends itself to being tackled in two days of more or less equal length with the first, hard day ending in Llanymynech. However, for those who do not want to cover the whole route in one or two days, the route description is divided into short sections. This makes it possible to choose a single section or combination of sections instead. Approximate distances are included for each section as well as a total distance from the beginning of the walk at the Lion Quays.

For those attempting the whole walk in a single day, it will come as a welcome relief to reach the village of Llanymynech at the southern end of the route where there's a chance to stock up and take a break. By the time you get there, you will have covered just over half the distance but the most difficult terrain will be behind you. The remaining 16 miles are almost entirely flat. Furthermore, the eastern section ahead of you offers a number of potential opportunites to buy food and drink.

If you intend to walk the Oswestry Round in sections, remember that the route is described as though it is to be attempted as one continuous walk. Be sure to check your starting point and your initial direction of travel carefully before you set off. It may help to look at the end of the section which precedes the one you are about to walk. Try to imagine the way ahead from the point of view of someone who has just completed the previous section.

Planning your walk

Planning your adventure in advance is part of the fun. It always brings rewards too. The information provided in the route description should be enough to get you round but we recommend you use this booklet in conjunction with the relevant Ordnance Survey map. The entire route is included on Landranger Map 126 covering Oswestry (1:50 000 scale) and also on the more detailed Explorer Map 240 for Oswestry (1:25 000 scale). A good map not only enables you to plan the route before you attempt it but also provides a bigger picture of the surrounding countryside as you walk. During your walk, you should check your position on the map regularly in order to be sure of your whereabouts. There is a sketch map on the centre pages of this booklet but remember that its purpose is only to give you a general idea of the route.

Access

The whole of the Oswestry Round is on public rights of way or permissive paths and there should be no access problems at any point along the route. If you encounter any difficulties or obstacles or if you would like to let us have your comments and suggestions please see the 'Contact Us' section.

Public transport

There are bus services from Oswestry to the start and end of most of the sections of the Oswestry Round. The nearest railway station to Oswestry is at Gobowen which is well served by trains from both the Chester and Shrewsbury directions. From Gobowen it is a two-mile ride into Oswestry by bus or taxi if you wish to go into town before starting your walk. It is one and a half miles from Gobowen to the start of the walk at the Lion Quays but currently there is no bus service to the Lion Quays. Further information on public transport in the Oswestry area can be found at www.traveline.info and www.traveline.cymru

Accommodation

The Oswestry Round starts and ends at the Lion Quays Hotel and Spa complex (www.lionquays.co.uk) just off the A5 to the north of Oswestry. The Lion Quays welcomes those attempting the Oswestry Round and there is ample parking, as well as food and a bed for the night. A range of accommodation types is available in the area, from camping to luxury hotels. You will find details of our sponsors at the back of this booklet. The Bradford Arms Hotel and Restaurant provides food and accommodation in the village of Llanymynech, at the half way point of the Oswestry Round. There is a Tourist Information office in the Heritage Centre in the middle of Oswestry (01691 662753) and also on the A5 at Mile End as you approach Oswestry from Shrewsbury (01691 662488). Much of the western section of the Oswestry Round follows Offa's Dyke Path, a popular National Trail. For accommodation suggestions contact the Offa's Dyke Association (www.offasdyke.demon.co.uk/bandb.htm). For further accommodation ideas visit our website www.oswestryround.co.uk

A few important things to consider

This is a very long and strenuous walk to undertake in a single day. You will obviously be able to enjoy it more if you're used to walking and have already done a number of long walks in preparation. If, on the day, the distance proves too great, remember that it is always best to stop. There will be other days, after all.

We've already mentioned the fun to be had in planning your walk and looking at the route on a map to become familiar with it. Planning pays dividends on long walks. It can be very frustrating to be unsure of your whereabouts, particularly as you grow more tired towards the end of a long day.

Although the route does not reach particularly high ground, remember that it can be colder and windier the higher you climb. It's important to have adequate clothing and suitable footwear. Always check the weather forecast too and be prepared to abandon your walk if conditions deteriorate.

Take plenty of provisions, including emergency rations. Don't rely on shops and pubs being open in rural locations. Check their opening times in advance if you intend to make use of them on your walk. Remember that, although you will never be more than a few miles from town, you will be passing through some quite remote countryside. This is true of the lower, eastern section as well as the higher, western one.

Unless you intend to carry enough food and drink for the whole day, decide in advance where you will be able to stock up or be met by friends who are supporting your effort. The route description may help to some extent as it refers to a number of places where food and drink can be bought and where cars can be parked. However, you musn't rely on this guide alone in this respect.

Particularly if you intend to walk on your own, you should let someone know where you are going before you set off and what time they should expect you back. Don't rely solely on mobile phones as reception can be unreliable.

GPS technology has improved vastly but in our view it is best never to rely entirely on any gadget which itself relies on batteries. There's no substitute for the ability to read a map and use a compass.

As you walk, get into the habit of making a mental note of the last place you passed where you could go for help if it's needed. Keep up to date too with your position on the route and with your location on the map, if you have one, rather than relying on someone else to guide you. It always pays to be self-sufficient in matters such as navigation, equipment and provisions.

Don't underestimate the eastern section even though it's virtually flat. You will grow increasingly tired as the miles wear on.

If you intend to take your dog into the countryside, it should be on a lead. On no account should it be allowed to annoy sheep, cattle or other walkers. In all other ways too, do follow the Countryside Code. It is mainly just good common sense, designed to help us all to respect, protect and enjoy our countryside. You can easily find the Code on-line, but here are its main points:

The Countryside Code
Respect, Protect, Enjoy

Respect other people

- Consider the local community and other people enjoying the outdoors
- Leave gates and property as you find them and follow paths unless wider access is available

Protect the natural environment

- Leave no trace of your visit and take your litter home
- Keep dogs under effective control

Enjoy the outdoors

- Plan ahead and be prepared
- Follow advice and local signs

Contact Us

Routes change from time to time. If you have any information or views you would like to share with us, please contact us via email - dand103750@aol.com

Offa's Dyke and Offa's Dyke Path (ODP)

Offa's Dyke - this is the earthwork which once formed the boundary between Wales and England and still does so in places. On some parts of the Oswestry Round the Dyke is clear to see. Elsewhere it is less obvious and in some places it cannot be seen at all. Stretches of Offa's Dyke lie on private ground with no public access.

Offa's Dyke Path - this is a National Trail running 177 miles from Prestatyn to Chepstow. It's important to remember that it does not always run alongside Offa's Dyke itself. On some parts of the Oswestry Round, Offa's Dyke Path deviates from the line of Offa's Dyke. ODP is one of the UK's most popular National Trails. Like all National Trails it is marked by an acorn symbol along the route. On this particular route, these are sometimes painted black or white.

The Oswestry Round

Section	Distance	Total distance
The Lion Quays to Craignant	4.9	4.9
Craignant to The Old Racecourse	2.9	7.8
The Old Racecourse to Trefonen	3.0	10.8
Trefonen to Nantmawr	2.3	13.1
Nantmawr to Llanymynech	3.9	17.0
Llanymynech to Maesbury Marsh	4.4	21.4
Maesbury Marsh to Queen's Head	2.2	23.6
Queen's Head to Lower Frankton	4.0	27.6
Lower Frankton to the Lion Quays	5.4	33

The Lion Quays to Craignant

Distance: 4.9 miles

The Oswestry Round begins at the Lion Quays Hotel and Spa complex. From the Lion Quays car park, turn right along the canalside path away from the buildings and the sound of the busy A5. This path takes you through trees and out onto a lane. Here, go left to the junction. Cross the canal bridge (number 16W) and descend immediately left to the towpath on the opposite side of the canal from where you started. Now walk back past the Lion Quays and pass below the A5 at bridge 17W. It will be another 23 miles until you reach the A5 once again at Queen's Head.

The next bridge you reach (18W) is on the edge of the village of Weston Rhyn. Continue along the canal towpath until you come to bridge 19W by the Poachers Pocket pub. This is where you leave the canal until you pick it up again in Llanymynech, still many miles away. Leave the towpath and cross the bridge. You will now follow paths and country lanes as you climb gradually to join Offa's Dyke Path (ODP) at the end of this first section of the Oswestry Round.

Continue along the lane to the edge of the hamlet of Chirk Bank. Immediately after the speed restriction signs, turn left along a track in front of houses. Stay on this until it narrows into a path which shortly brings you into Oliver's Wood. At the information board for Oliver's Wood turn right along a path through the trees. Follow this path until you reach a short rise onto a low bank ahead. Climb onto the bank and turn right along it to reach a stile on the edge of the wood. Once over this stile, ignore a path (sometimes not obvious) going off to the right. Instead, with your back to the stile you've just crossed, look more or less straight ahead across the field for a stile by tall trees about 150 yards away. Cross the field to this stile, go over it and follow the path beyond. This path leads to another stile. You then join a lane between houses and soon you reach the road at Chirk Bank.

Cross the road and enter Trehowell Avenue. Continue along this lane for nearly half a mile until you reach a T-junction. Turn right and after a few yards go over a stile on the left by a hollow oak tree. Now climb straight ahead past farm buildings to a stile just left of the highest point you can see. Once over the stile, continue with the field boundary on your right. Cross another stile and drop slightly to pass through a tunnel and emerge directly onto a road. Go left along the road for a few yards until you see a stile by a gate on the right. Cross this stile. From here, aim just to the right of the solitary tree high in the field, a little below the wood on the hilltop (Temple Wood). Ahead you will find a stile which leads into the wood. Cross the stile and, almost immediately, pass through another tunnel. Keep going to reach another stile. Cross this and leave the wood.

At this point, trend slightly to the right of the top of the rise ahead. (Look left for a view of the Stonehenge replica in the distance which gives this wood its name). Now head downhill through the field, aiming just to the right of the two big trees in a line below you, towards a stile in the field boundary. Go over this stile to emerge straight onto another road. Cross this road and follow the lane opposite. Pass below a bridge and at the T-junction go left. Ignore the next left turn you come to. Carry on gently uphill until you reach the next turning on your left. Take this left turn. This lane rises gradually to a T-junction at Dinas Cottage. Now turn right, uphill.

Stay on the lane which eventually levels out at a sharp left bend. (Ignore the track which joins you from the right at this point). The lane soon starts to drop slightly to reach a point where it bends sharply to the right and starts to climb once more.

This short steep section has fine views over to the left towards the Shropshire Hills. Once again, the lane levels out and then reaches a crossroads. Turn right uphill. The lane you are now on soon steepens but eventually, just around a left bend, it levels out near a triangle of grass where two more lanes meet it, one from the right and then one from the left. Ignore these two side lanes and stay on the main lane.

As you continue along your lane, the valley carrying Morlas Brook starts to appear on your left. Gradually you lose height and meet the brook itself. Just beyond a house opposite a converted chapel, the lane climbs steeply left. Shortly, you emerge onto the Oswestry-Glyn Ceiriog road (B4579) at Craignant at a point where you see an Offa's Dyke Path (ODP) sign for the first time. This is where you pick up ODP which you will be following for several miles, almost as far as Llanymynech, the village which marks the southernmost point of the Oswestry Round. ODP is well-signposted so keep your eyes open for the signs and for the acorn symbol which denotes a National Trail, sometimes painted black or white.

(For anyone walking the Oswestry Round in sections and relying on private transport, there is a convenient place to park cars just a short distance to the right along the B4579.)

Craignant to the Old Racecourse

Distance: 2.9 miles (total 7.8 miles)

From the point where you climbed to reach the B4579 at the end of the previous section, turn right along the road for a few yards and then take a rising track on the left signposted Selattyn Hill. Notice the acorn symbol which tells you that you are on Offa's Dyke Path (ODP). You will be following ODP throughout this section. Follow this broad track uphill to reach a gate at a point where the track itself swings sharp left. Go through this gate onto another track which provides access to Woodside cottage. Proceed between lines of trees and eventually pass Woodside, which is over to your right. Continue uphill alongside the remains of a stone wall to reach another gate and a stile.

Go through the gate or over the stile. After about 50 yards trend left uphill, as indicated by a finger post. Go up and over the brow of the hill to reach a stile and ODP sign. Cross the stile. Now take the track to the right which leads you gently downhill for over a third of a mile - passing through three gates along the way - until it eventually runs out at a point where it climbs left to join an access track to a farm. Go right for a few yards along this better track and then cross a stile on the left to enter a small field. Another stile then takes you into a larger field and after a third stile you drop towards a footbridge over a stream. Cross the footbridge and climb to reach a good section of Offa's Dyke itself. Keep Offa's Dyke on your right as you proceed south through fields, then along the edge of a plantation and finally through more fields until you eventually emerge onto the road at Carreg-y-big.

Turn right along this road and after about 100 yards turn left along another road signposted to Oswestry Racecourse. Stay on this road for almost a mile, ignoring any left turns, until you drop gently to a staggered crossroads at the Oswestry-Llansilin road (B4580). Cross the road. Here, an ODP sign points the way ahead to Candy Wood. A series of posts with the acorn symbol now directs you straight ahead across the common, where horse races were held until 1848, until you reach the ruin of the grandstand at the highest point.

(For anyone walking the Oswestry Round in sections and relying on private transport, there is a car park over to the left as you approach the grandstand.)

The Old Racecourse to Trefonen

Distance: 3.0 miles (total 10.8 miles)

Being lost in a wood is no fun, so it's particularly important to look out for Offa's Dyke Path (ODP) signs as you pass through Candy Wood at the beginning of this section. Remain alert and don't be drawn off-course by other signs or other paths. You will be following ODP all the way to Trefonen.

From the grandstand at the Old Racecourse, carry on in the same direction (i.e. roughly south, away from the Oswestry-Llansilin road) keeping the small statue of a two-headed horse to your left. Go downhill through the wood. Emerge briefly where a field appears on your left. When you re-enter the wood take the main, lower path downhill. You now climb to the right onto the Dyke itself. Stay on it for a short distance until a signpost directs you to the right and you pass through a dip in the Dyke. ODP now swerves immediately left, keeping close to the Dyke. With the Dyke now on your left, proceed for some distance until, eventually, at a fork, an ODP sign directs you downhill (right fork). Carry on downhill until you reach a T-junction of paths. Go right for about 20 yards and then left downhill. You will soon reach another junction of paths. Take the lower of the two paths on the left, which goes downhill. Continue on this path until you emerge from the wood by a house. Go left along its drive which soon becomes a lane. Shortly afterwards, at a road junction, turn right to cross the river Morda and, shortly after this, turn left along another road.

The road soon starts to climb steeply. At the T-junction at the top of the hill, cross the road diagonally left and then cross a stile to follow ODP with the Dyke now on your right. Stay on this side of the Dyke for some distance until, eventually, you are directed by an ODP sign

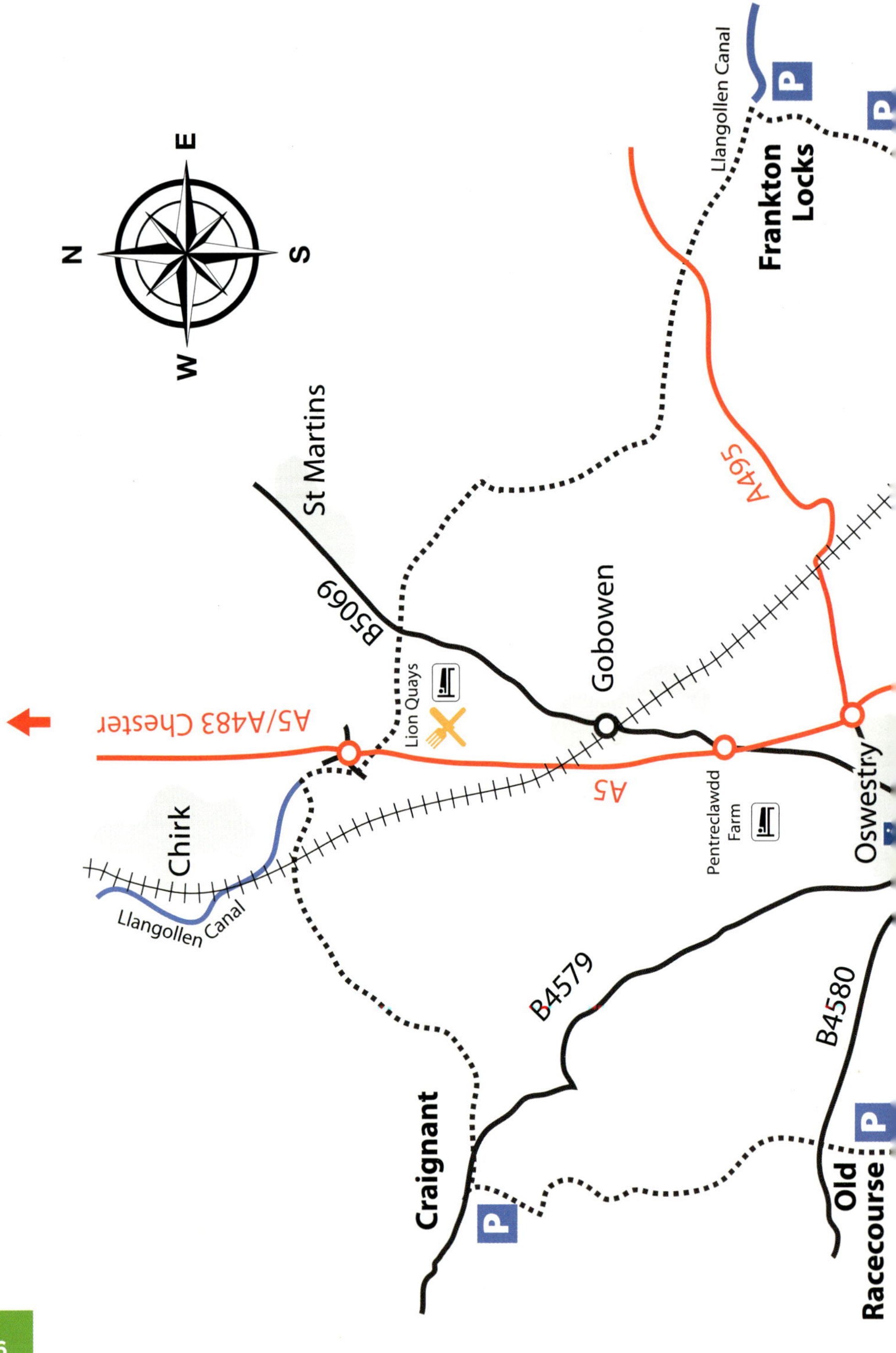
N
E
S
W
St Martins
B5069
Lion Quays
A5/A483 Chester
Gobowen
Chirk
Llangollen Canal
A5
Pentreclawdd Farm
Oswestry
A495
Frankton Locks
Llangollen Canal
B4579
B4580
Craignant
Old Racecourse
P

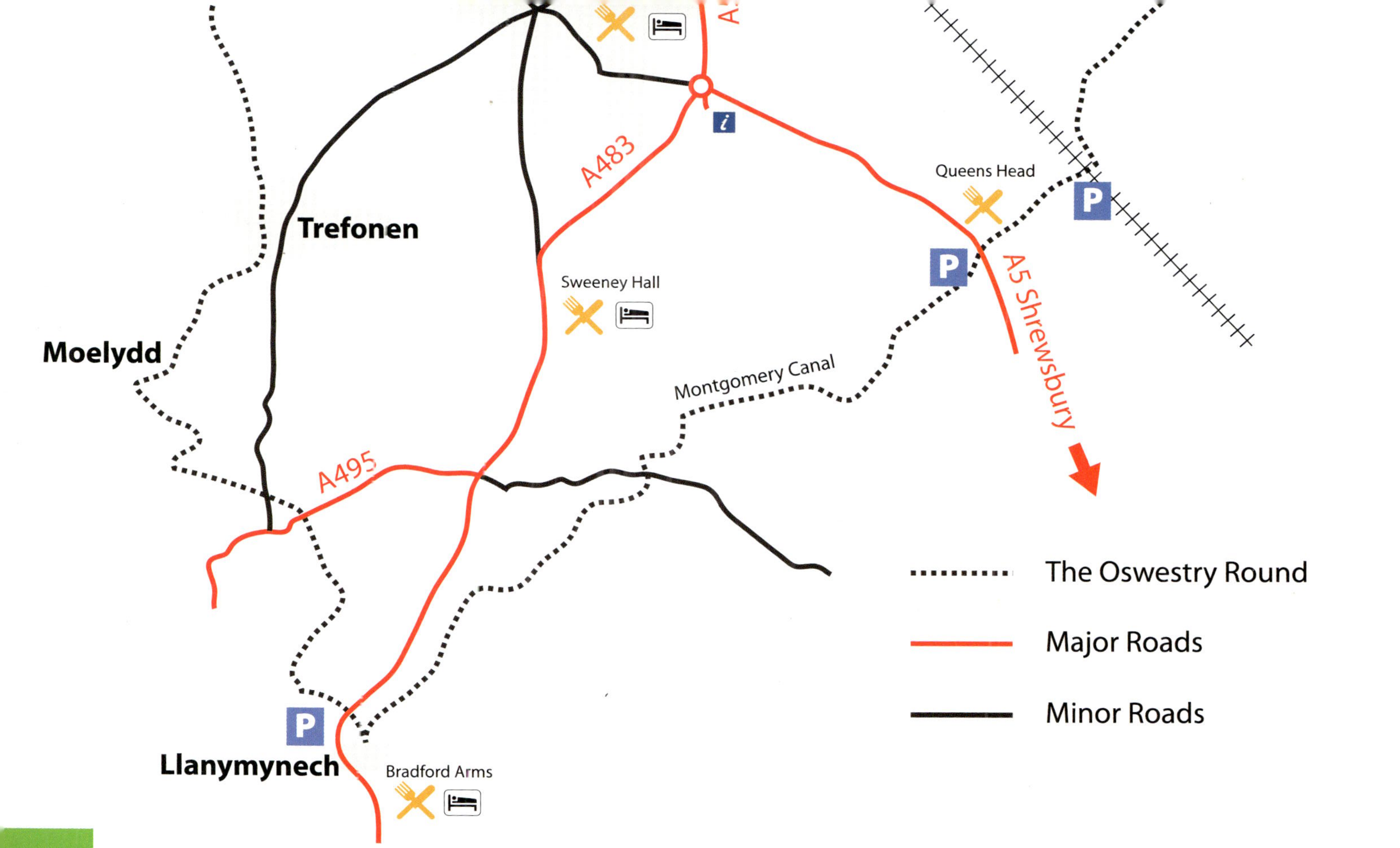

Trefonen
Moelydd
A483
Sweeney Hall
Queens Head
A5 Shrewsbury
Montgomery Canal
A495
Llanymynech
Bradford Arms
The Oswestry Round
Major Roads
Minor Roads

through a gap in the Dyke which you now follow on the opposite side until you reach a lane. Once on the lane do a left-right dog-leg to enter another field with the village of Trefonen in sight ahead. Follow the field boundary on your left until - about two thirds of the way down the field - another sign directs you to the right towards a farm. Take the broad track alongside the farm buildings to reach Trefonen. The track narrows into a path as you approach the village. Soon you emerge onto a road. This is Malthouse Lane. Go straight ahead along Malthouse Lane until you reach a T-junction. The Oswestry Round continues with a right turn here along Bellan Lane.

(For anyone walking the Oswestry Round in sections and relying on private transport, there is a small parking area near the main road to Oswestry which you would now reach by turning left instead of right along Bellan Lane. At the end of the lane, pass immediately in front of the Barley Mow pub to reach this parking area which is opposite the entrance to Whitridge Way (and just off Chapel Lane if you're approaching from the road to Oswestry) and is adjacent to the pub's own car park.)

Trefonen to Nantmawr

Distance: 2.3 miles (total 13.1 miles)

Throughout this section you will, once again, be following Offa's Dyke Path (ODP), so look out for the ODP signposts. From Malthouse Lane at the end of the previous section, go right along Bellan Lane. Stay on this lane until you reach a point where it bends sharp right. Leave the lane at this point and go directly ahead towards a field. Walk straight ahead into the field, keeping just left of the tree in front of you. Keep the

hedge on your right for some distance until eventually you reach a stile. Go over the stile and cross a stone slab bridge over a stream. Then cross a field straight ahead to another stile. Cross this and climb directly uphill towards a tree. From the tree, go straight ahead past more trees to a gate and emerge onto a lane. Here make a left-right dog-leg to pick up another lane.

Just around the first bend, ignore the left fork and stay on your lane. This soon passes through a farmyard where it bends to the left and reaches a gate. Continue through the gate and walk for some distance along the lane until you eventually reach a stile on your right (at the entrance to Tŷ Uchaf). Once over the stile, follow the hedge on your right all the way up to the farm above, ignoring the obvious left bend ahead in the track. Once at the gate to the farmyard, turn left along the track from the farm. You soon reach a junction of tracks where you need to fork right uphill. Keep climbing this stony track as it bends right and left uphill until you see a signpost at a left bend which directs you to the right, away from the track. Walk uphill through scrub and over open ground to the summit of Moelydd and its extensive views. Moelydd provides what is probably the best vantage point of the whole of the Oswestry Round.

Leave the summit in the direction shown by the signpost and follow other signposts as you descend to a track which goes left and soon passes an isolated house. When this track bends sharply to the left, go straight ahead on grass to reach a stile on the right, near an ODP sign. Cross this and go downhill. On your way down, you pass a ruin on your right and shortly afterwards you reach a gate. Once through the gate, go diagonally left. Soon you enter Jones' Rough Nature Reserve. Continue downhill all the way through the reserve, ignoring a path and stile to your left about half way down. When you emerge at the far end of the reserve, turn left along a track from a house which becomes a tarmac lane outside the next house. Go along this lane. Ignore the next right turn and in about 50 yards you reach a signpost on your right which points your way downhill through a field towards the hamlet of Nantmawr. Part way down, where the ground becomes less steep, look out for another sign which directs you left into a second field. Cross this field and then another field to reach a path between gardens which leads to the road at Nantmawr.

Nantmawr to Llanymynech

Distance: 3.9 miles (total 17.0 miles)

During this section you will be following Offa's Dyke Path (ODP) most of the way but when you reach the Shropshire border on the flanks of Llanymynech Hill, just before you drop towards the village of Llanymynech and your half way point, you will be leaving it. As in previous sections, look out for the ODP signposts as you proceed. Look out also for flying golf balls as you skirt the golf course on Llanymynech Hill!

From the point where you emerged onto the road at the end of the previous section, turn right downhill. Go down through the hamlet of Nantmawr, cross the bridge at the bottom and as the road climbs again look out for a stile on your left. Cross this, go briefly through trees and cross another stile into a field. Go up this field towards a farm to reach a lane. This is Cefn Lane. Go left along Cefn Lane for over half a mile, all the way to where it ends at a crossroads. (En route you will cross an old railway and another road will join you from the left.)

At the crossroads, go straight ahead into Coopers Lane. Soon another lane joins it from the left and a few yards later look out for a stile on your right which leads to a path between houses. This path leads down to a field which you cross, trending left half way down, to emerge a few yards from the A495 at Porth-y-waen. Cross the A495 diagonally left and walk along a tarmac drive. Just around the first bend in the drive, cross a stile on your left. Stay close to the fence on your right as it curves to the right towards a footbridge (don't be drawn to a more obvious footbridge away to your left). Once over the bridge, cross a field and then a railway line. Now,

cross two larger fields to reach a road by a wood. Go straight ahead uphill along the road. At the first right bend, go left along a track. This soon becomes a path which runs alongside a line of trees and then climbs to the right into the woods towards Llanymynech Hill.

Eventually you reach a crossroads of paths where you turn right along Offa's Dyke itself. The path continues through trees and then along the edge of the golf course atop Llanymynech Hill and back into trees again, following the line of Offa's Dyke. The Oswestry Round and ODP do not visit the actual summit of Llanymynech Hill but if you have the energy it is certainly worth making a detour for the splendid views. The point at which you can start your detour comes when your path emerges briefly from the trees and trends to the right, crossing another signposted path (a bridleway actually), towards a wooden gate beyond which you can see an information board (for Llanymynech Rocks). The Oswestry Round and ODP continue through this gate but if you want to detour to the summit of Llanymynech Hill read the next paragraph. Otherwise skip to the paragraph which follows it.

<u>Detour to the top of Llanymynech Hill</u> - Instead of going through the gate, turn left uphill along the bridleway and climb briefly through trees until you emerge on the edge of a fairway. You will soon see a concrete trig point above you to your right. Reaching this trig point

would involve crossing the fairway and you should watch out for flying golf balls and avoid causing annoyance to golfers. But the best view, anyway, is actually to be had from another rise further to your right. Reach this by following the edge of the fairway. The views are excellent. There is a bench and a good topograph. Now return by the same route to the point where you left the Oswestry Round and ODP.

Oswestry Round continued - Once through the gate and beyond the information board for Llanymynech Rocks, ODP - which you are still following for the time being - now curves left below the rocks towards the village of Llanymynech. There are open views ahead and to your right. At this point you are in Wales, though not for long. Stick carefully to ODP now as there are several other paths in this area which could draw you off course. However, when you reach the ruin of the Welsh Brake Drum House on your left (which has an information board) get ready to leave ODP.

A short distance beyond the Welsh Brake Drum House, as you re-enter England (Shropshire), ODP itself turns sharp right, descends steeply through trees and leads eventually to Llanymynech. Instead, go straight ahead on the upper path. This soon drops to the ruin of the English Brake Drum House (which also has an information board). Here, turn right and follow the incline plane downhill, ignoring side paths, until your way is blocked by a sudden drop ahead of you. Ignoring the path to the right, skirt left around trees. Soon you pass below the A483 and enter the Llanymynech Heritage Area. As you enter the Heritage Area, pass a house on your left and bear right to cross a brook just before the first ruin (the Tally House). The main attraction in the Heritage Area is the splendid Hoffman Kiln which is signposted to the left and requires a short but worthwhile detour.

The main track through the Heritage Area now leads you to the Limeworks Stables with its Education Room. Just ahead, you will see the canal for the first time since you left it at the Poachers Pocket pub. You will be seeing a lot more of it from now on!

Just beyond the Limeworks Stables, turn right along a track which brings you into the Heritage Area car park. From here, go up to the A483 and turn left towards the centre of Llanymynech. Perhaps it's time for a rest!

Llanymynech to Maesbury Marsh

Distance: 4.4 miles (total 21.4 miles)

At Llanymynech you're at the southernmost point of the Oswestry Round. You have walked 17 of the 33 miles. The harder, hilly section is now behind you and you can look forward to much easier walking on the remainder of the route as it is almost entirely flat. It follows the course of the old and now partially restored Montgomery Canal all the way to its junction with the Llangollen Canal at Lower Frankton and then follows this latter canal all the way back to the Lion Quays and the end of your adventure.

In this section we will be referring occasionally to canal bridge numbers and it's important to keep your eyes open for these as you proceed. They appear on both sides of each bridge. Please don't assume that all you have to do is follow the canal. In certain places along the route, it would be easy to make a mistake. This is particularly true early on as the canal has not currently been restored all the way down to Llanymynech and is dry in places. Some bridges have also been removed or have fallen into disrepair.

Even when you reach the restored section it would still be a mistake to lose concentration.

From the road bridge in Llanymynech, drop to the canal's south side, the side nearest the village centre. Turn right along the canal path (if you turn left you could end up in Newtown!). You should now have the canal on your left. As you proceed, the tall chimney of the Hoffman Kiln comes into view across the canal which soon ends abruptly. For about three miles you will now be following the course of the canal which, at the time of writing, has not been fully restored.

The course of the canal continues through trees. The way ahead is clear. When you pass below bridge 90 go straight ahead on a path and not on the minor road to its right. You will see a row of lime kilns to your left. Soon, at an old quarry, you have to climb steps and then drop down the far side to regain the canal path.

The wide path continues through trees, then past houses and then once more through trees, still with a lane below you on the right. The remains of the canal are now little more than a shallow depression on your left.

After bridge 88 continue on your embankment with standing water and vegetation visible in the canal. The view on your right gradually opens out as you proceed and you will see the Breidden Hills with the local landmark of Rodney's Pillar. Beyond bridge 87 the view opens up on both sides.

Soon the path climbs to cross a minor road. The course of the old canal is quite clear ahead as you continue with it still to your left. Between bridges 85 and 84 you pass a large industrial unit and you also pass the point the restoration work on the canal has currently reached on its way to Llanymynech.

Now that you have reached the restored section of the canal, route-finding may seem much easier. You may be tempted to lose concentration and merely follow the water. But stay alert! You won't want to make a mistake this far into your walk. At bridge 80 you reach Canal Central where there is a tearoom and shop. It's now only a short distance to the next bridge (79) at Maesbury Marsh and the Navigation Inn.

Maesbury Marsh to Queen's Head

Distance: 2.2 miles (total 23.6 miles)

A fine stretch of canal now leads through very pleasant countryside, often with extensive views both left and right, for a mile and a quarter to Aston Locks. Beyond the last of the locks and the nearby nature reserve you reach the busy A5 at Queen's Head. Pass below the A5 (bridge 76A) and almost immediately go under the Queen's Head bridge (76).

(For anyone walking the Oswestry Round in sections and relying on private transport, there is a car park opposite the Queen's Head where the upper area is available to the public.)

Queen's Head to Lower Frankton

Distance: 4.0 miles (total 27.6 miles)

For just under a mile (0.9 miles) beyond Queen's Head bridge (76), the canal runs alongside a minor road to reach bridge 74. Pass below this bridge and then cross it to continue on the opposite side of the canal which now passes below the railway line to Shrewsbury (bridge 73) and bends north, away from the road. (There is a car park just down the lane opposite bridge 74.)

Away to your left you have the hills of the western section of the Oswestry Round. After a little over half a mile, the canal swings slightly right to reveal a straight but pleasant section which stretches almost a mile ahead to the aqueduct over the river Perry. Beyond the river, the canal continues through pleasant countryside to reach the Graham Palmer lock and commemorative stone. Shortly afterwards you pass below bridge 70, the last one on the Montgomery Canal. A sharp left bend in the canal leads you to Frankton Locks where the Montgomery Canal meets the Llangollen Canal.

(For anyone walking the Oswestry Round in sections and relying on private transport, there are two car parks near the end of this section, both on the east side of the canal. One is at the canal junction at Lower Frankton and the other half a mile to the south.)

Lower Frankton to the Lion Quays

Distance: 5.4 miles (total 33.0 miles)

Turn left along the Llangollen Canal, now heading north-west. This is an important point in your long walk as you turn towards the end with just 5.4 miles to go. Pass below bridge 1W and continue on this side of the canal until you reach bridge 3W which you cross to reach the north bank. When you pass below the main A495 between Oswestry and Ellesmere at bridge 5W you will see the Narrow Boat Inn on the opposite bank. At

bridge 6W, cross back to the south bank of the canal. After you pass below bridge 11W you arrive at the Jack Mytton Inn. From here the canal turns north and in a little over a mile you reach the top lock at New Marton, having already passed the bottom lock on your way. Just beyond the top lock, cross New Marton bridge (bridge 12W) to continue on the opposite side of the canal.

You now have less than two miles to go and the hills you climbed during the early stages of the Oswestry Round seem close once again. It's time to start counting down the bridges! There are only four to go. It is just over a mile to the next one (13W) at St Martin's Moor which carries the road from Oswestry to St Martin's (B5069). The next bridge (Sarn Bridge - 14W) connects farmland at Sarn Farm and the one after (Preeshenlle Bridge - 15W) carries a public footpath (part of Wat's Dyke Way Heritage Trail). There is now just one bridge to go. This is bridge 16W which you crossed at the beginning of your walk. Pass under bridge 16W and climb to the right to leave the canal towpath. You are almost back at the Lion Quays where your long walk began. Cross the bridge, turn right along a lane and, staying with the canal, take a path through trees on the right. This brings you back to the car park at the Lion Quays.

Congratulations! It's time to relax and celebrate, surely.

AA
Hotel
Certificate of Excellence